ABRA·CA·DAZZLE:
EASY MAGIC TRICKS

Ray Broekel and Laurence B. White, Jr.

Illustrated by Mary Thelen

ALBERT WHITMAN & COMPANY, MORTON GROVE, ILLINOIS

*This book is dedicated to all the rabbits
that live in magicians' hats. May
they increase and multiply!*

12   11   10   9   8   7   6   5
Text © 1982 by Ray Broekel and Laurence B. White, Jr.
Illustrations © 1982 by Mary Thelen.
Published in 1982 by Albert Whitman & Company,
6340 Oakton Street, Morton Grove, Illinois 60053.
Published simultaneously in Canada by
General Publishing, Limited, Toronto.

Library of Congress Cataloging-in-Publication Data
Broekel, Ray.
    Abra-ca-dazzle: easy magic tricks.
    Summary: Explains basic principles of magic and
gives directions for twenty-five easy magic tricks.
    1. Tricks—Juvenile literature. 2. Conjuring—
Juvenile literature. [1. Magic tricks.] I. White,
Laurence B. II. Thelen, Mary, ill. III. Title.
GV1548.B7   793.8   81-11578
ISBN 0-8075-0121-2   AACR2

*The body of this book is set in 12 point Helvetica Regular.
The heads are in 36 and 18 point Italia Medium.*

CONTENTS

GETTING STARTED

Magic is fun. But it takes practicing magic is fun, too. Do it in front of a mirror. When you can fool yourself, you can fool your friends.

As you read this book you will first learn tricks that are easy to do. Then the tricks will get harder and you will find you need more practice. Professional magicians are able to cut people in half, float them in air, and pull rabbits out of hats. Imagine how much practice those tricks take!

Before you begin to do the tricks in this book, you should start thinking like a magician. Study each trick you wish to do. There is a secret to every one. Figure out what it is. You must keep the secret hidden from your audience.

Ask yourself some questions. Must you do the trick fast or slow? Must you keep some object or action hidden from view? Is the trick better when it is performed for one person or a group of people? Should you do it close to your audience or far away?

For example, tricks with thread work best if you're not too close to your audience. If you stand too close, everyone will see the thread and you will look silly. You can choose the tricks you will show partly by

EVEN A SMALL CHILD CAN DO THIS TRICK AS WELL AS I CAN—AFTER YEARS OF PRACTICE.

figuring out how many people will be in your audience and how close they will be to you.

As you do magic, you must think constantly of your audience. What do they see? What do you want them to think they see?

Suppose you want people to think you have an object in your left hand, but you actually don't. How can you make your left hand look as though it contains something? You must learn to hold your left hand slightly open, with the back toward your audience. You must look at your left hand and act as though something is in it. The best magicians are those who learn to ACT.

A good magician can make people look where he wants them to. How? By asking. By looking. By pointing. By making a sound. If you snap your fingers, people will look at your fingertips. If you stare at your empty hand, people will look at it, too. If you point in one direction, people will look where your finger points. If you ask people to look at something closely, chances are they will. Getting people to look in the wrong place is called *misdirection*. It is one

MY WAND iS MADE OF GUMWOOD—— It's fOUND UNDER DESK TOPS.

I AM THE WORLD'S MOST FAMOUS GIZZARD — OOPS! I MEAN WIZARD.

of a magician's greatest secrets. As you learn more and more about the art of magic, you will learn to use your actions and your voice to make people look exactly where you want them to.

How about your patter? That's what a magician says. What are you going to say as you perform your tricks? You might choose funny patter:

> *For this trick I need the help of ten of my oldest friends ... my fingers. I really couldn't do without them ... In fact, I've had them since I was a small child. With their help I will do this simply awful trick ...* NO. NO, *I mean awfully simple trick. I'll also need this little white ball that I have colored* RED. . . .

Or you can just tell the audience what's happening: "For my next trick I will use these two paper cups and a tiny red ball. Keep your eye on the RED ball while I drop it into the first cup. . . ."

Be sure to use some patter. People like to hear tricks as well as see them. And, remember, practice your patter whenever you practice your tricks.

Think about your costume. It doesn't have to be a black suit and tall hat, but sometimes you do need special clothing, like long sleeves or open cuffs or dark-colored jeans or big pockets to hold and hide special things. As you do the tricks in this book, you will be able to figure out the clothing you will need. Then you will pick the right costume—the clothing that will help you.

What happens if you follow all the directions and practice and a trick still fails? Relax! Don't take yourself too seriously. If a trick goes wrong, just grin and say, "I guess you caught me that time," and then immediately proceed to your next trick. You will be surprised. People will not remember that you failed. They will only remember the tricks that worked and fooled them. The only person who will remember the tricks that didn't work is YOU, the magician.

Finally, remember that a magician's most important job is to entertain other people. Please try every one of these tricks on your friends—even the tricks you don't think you will like. You may get a big surprise. Your friends may like the ones you don't. Learn the tricks other people like best and do those. Then you'll be a very popular magician!

HMMMMM—
NO RABBit?

i JUSt DiD tHAt
to See if you weRe
PAYiNG AtteNtioN.

TEACH YOUR FRIENDS A LESSON

The Trick

An audience is in front of you. You say, "Are you ready?" Your audience will be eager to learn the new trick you are going to explain.

You remove a piece of paper and a pencil from your pocket. You say, "I am going to show you how to make a pear disappear. Are you ready?" Your audience will be anxious to learn the new trick you are going to show. On the paper you print: PEAR.

Now you explain, "I shall make the pear disappear. All it takes is a D, an I, an S, an A, and a P." You write these letters in front of PEAR. "I have made the PEAR disappear," you proudly say. And you finish by saying, "I began by promising to teach you a lesson. And I have. The lesson is to never trust a magician!"

disappear

(NEVER TRUST A MAGICIAN.)

The Trick

Hand a friend a small box and say, "This box contains my assistant—a teeny, weeny genie." Your friend will be puzzled. "Would you like to see it?" you ask. "Yes," your friend will probably answer.

Ask the other people present, "Do you think my friend will see it?" "No," at least one person will answer, thinking you are being silly.

Have your friend open the box and peek inside. You say, "Now be honest. Tell us if you see it." Your friend must honestly answer, "Yes."

Here's How

This is just a fun trick. It lets you and your friend fool the audience . . . honestly. Your friend won't really see a genie inside the box, but your friend will see IT. Inside the box you have placed a slip of paper. On it you have printed the word IT. When you ask if your friend sees IT, he will have to say, "Yes." You can then let your audience see IT. People will probably laugh, and making people laugh is an important part of a magician's job.

THE TEENY WEENY GENIE

THIS BOX HAS five SIDES—
A BACKSIDE,
fRONTSIDE,
TOPSIDE,
BOTTOMSIDE AND
INSIDE.

PICK A COLOR, ANY COLOR

i will SNAP MY fingers Twice! That will make this Trick twice as snappy... now, without looking i will tell you the color of this crayon behind my back.

The Trick

Give a friend a handful of colored crayons. Turn your back to him and hold out your hand behind you. "Place any color of crayon in my hand," you say, "and hide the rest." He does this, and you turn to face him. Your hand is still behind your back. You pretend to concentrate. You turn your back to your friend again and hold up the crayon behind you. You still cannot see it. "Please concentrate on the color," you say. He does. "It is YELLOW," you say. And it is! Do the trick again, using another color. And again if you wish.

Here's How

Stand near an old table when you do this trick. After taking the crayon from your friend, turn around and face him. The hand with the crayon should now be behind your back and close to the table. Make a tiny crayon mark on the edge of the table. Then turn around and face the table again. Your friend will see the crayon. You will see the mark on the edge of the table. Now you can name the color of the crayon. (Crayon marks won't hurt the table, but do wipe them off when you are finished. That way no one will learn your secret.)

The Trick

You say to someone, "I'm going to give you a test to see if you can watch carefully." You hold up a small paper bag, a playing card, and a penny. You drop the card and the penny into the bag. Then you reach in, remove the card, and drop it into your pocket. "What is in the bag?" you ask. "The penny," will probably be the person's answer.

"No," you say. "The penny is here in my pocket." You remove the penny from your pocket. Of course, the person will reach for the bag. What does he find inside? Just the card!

Here's How

This is the secret. Put an extra playing card in the bag before you begin. Do not show the inside of the bag. Drop the penny and the card into the bag. Reach in and take out one of the cards. At the same time, take out the penny but keep it hidden underneath the card. Drop them both into your pocket. Later take the penny out of your pocket and show it to the person. Let him take the card out of the bag.

WHAT'S WHERE? WATCH IT!

SESTPRO! -OOPS!
TESTROP! -OOPS!
I'M SORRY, I'VE NEVER
BEEN ABLE TO SAY PRESTO.

(PRESTO?)

11

THE MYSTERIOUS MIND READER

The Trick

Three paper plates are right-side-up on a table. You turn them over one at a time and show your audience that each plate has a different colored bottom. Now place the plates back right-side-up on the table and move them around quickly. When you stop, nobody should know which color is where. Stand with your back to the plates and ask someone to pick up any plate to see what color is on the bottom. Then have the person put the plate back where it was. Turn around. You pick up the same plate that the person has chosen!

Here's How

Make a tiny pencil mark on the edge of each plate. Only you will know the marks are there. After you hold up the plates, put them back on the table. Scramble them, but when you stop, make certain that the secret marks all face the same direction. Turn your back to the plates. Nobody will know which color is where—not even you.

The person you call on will turn over one plate to see its color and then put it back. When you turn around you still won't know what colored plates are where. But you will know which secret mark is now in a different place. The plate with the out-of-place mark must be the one that was picked up! Flip it over and say, "You chose the red (or whatever color you now see) plate!"

AND NOW FOR A BONUS MIND-READING TRICK:

WRITE A WORD ON A PIECE OF PAPER AND STEP ON it! I CAN TELL YOU WHAT'S ON it— YOUR FOOT!

THE ACE OF TOES

The Trick

Ask your audience, "Do you know why the Ace of Hearts is sometimes called the 'Ace of Toes'?" You place a deck of cards on the floor face down.

"It's because you can find the Ace of Hearts with your toes," you answer. "Let me show you how."

You remove one of your shoes and wiggle your toes. Then you start pushing against the side of the cards with your toes. You push a little harder. Suddenly the deck splits apart. You turn the top part over and show the bottom card to your audience. There is the Ace of Hearts. You shout, "The Ace of Toes!"

Here's How

Salt!

Before your audience arrives, remove the Ace of Hearts from a deck of cards. Then divide the deck into two equal parts. Put half of the deck face down on a flat surface. Put a pinch of table salt on the top card. Then put the Ace of Hearts face down on top of the salt, and put the other half of the deck on top of the Ace of Hearts.

CHA-KA-ZOOP-
ALA-ZIMBA-BAM!

When you are ready to perform the trick, pick up the deck carefully and set it face down on the floor. No one will be able to tell that you've put salt on one of the cards. Give the deck a push forward with your toes. The salt will make the deck split right at the Ace of Hearts. Let the salt fall off as you pick up the cards. Then your friends won't be able to do the trick or discover your secret.

FOR THIS TRICK, I CALL UPON THE HELP OF MY TEN FAMOUS FRIENDS... MY TOES... AS I WIGGLE THEM, WILL SOMEONE IN THE AUDIENCE PLEASE SAY THE MAGIC WORD?

(DILL PICKLE!)

THE JUMP-BACK CARDS

The Trick

Remove two cards from the top of a deck and show them to your audience. Explain, "These are called 'jump-back' cards. I'll show you why."

Push the two cards into the deck in different places. Then tap the top of the deck and say, "Okay, jump back!" You turn over the two cards on top, and the first two cards have jumped back to where they were!

Here's How

The two cards you remove from the deck at the beginning of the trick are NOT the same cards you show at the end. Before your

DO YOU KNOW
ONE CARD FROM ANOTHER?

(WHAT'S THE OTHER?)

16

audience arrives, put the Five of Clubs and the Four of Spades on top of the deck. Put the Four of Clubs and the Five of Spades on top of the first two cards.

The first cards you show your audience are the Four of Clubs and the Five of Spades. Show them QUICKLY, and do NOT say their names. Just flash them at your audience as you say, "These are called 'jump-back' cards." Immediately push them into the deck. After tapping the top of the deck and giving the command to "jump back," you turn over the two cards that are now on top—the Five of Clubs and the Four of Spades. Do you think anyone will remember that they are not the same cards as the ones you first showed?

Most people won't remember. If one of your friends is really sharp and does remember, just say, "I was only checking to make sure you were watching carefully." Then quickly go on to another trick.

OH, BROTHER!

THE CASE OF THE MISSING COINS

The Trick

Shake your fist back and forth. Coins jingle inside. Ask a friend, "Will you hold these coins?" Your friend reaches to take them. You open your hand. ZAP. Your hand is empty!

Here's How

There never were any coins in your hand. This trick uses a strange secret: sound. You need to wear a long-sleeved shirt or blouse. Drop some coins into a small plastic sandwich bag. Slip two rubber bands around your forearm as close to your wrist as possible. Put the top of the bag under the top rubber band and the bottom of the bag under the bottom band. The coins should be in the middle. Pull down your shirt sleeve to hide the rubber bands and bag. Shake your arm, not just your fist, when you perform the trick.

Listen. The hidden coins will jingle inside the bag. They will sound like they are in your fist. Keep your fist closed until your friend reaches for the coins. Open your fist. The coins will seem to vanish into thin air. (Be careful not to shake your arm after you have opened your hand, or your audience will discover your secret.)

18

The Trick

Ask a friend to help you with this trick. Hold up a piece of paper and a pencil. Say, "Please think of any number. I will read your mind and write it on this piece of paper." Your friend thinks. You think. You write on the paper.

Say, "I think I have written the number you are thinking of. But there are lots of different numbers. Are you thinking of one yet?" Your friend answers, "Yes."

"Good!" you shout. "I knew you were thinking of ONE!" You hold the paper up to your audience. You have written the number *1* on it.

Here's How

There is no magic here, but the trick is fun anyway. Be sure to ask, "Are you thinking of ONE yet?" That makes YOUR answer right, even if it is not the number your friend thought of!

THINK OF ONE

THE THING UNDER THE TOWEL

The Trick

You open a large beach towel and show both sides to your audience. "Watch," you say as you drop the beach towel to the floor. The towel does not fall flat. A large bump is under it.

"Look," you say, "a miracle!" Pull the towel away to show a sneaker. "A SNEAKER," you shout. "Where did that come from?" After a moment the audience knows.

Here's How

Where did the sneaker come from? From your foot, of course. When you show the towel, make sure it hides your legs and feet from view. Behind the towel, slip out of one sneaker. Step backwards as you drop the towel over the shoe. At the same time hide your bare foot behind your other leg.

Pull the towel away to show the sneaker. Pretend to be amazed. Then slowly move your sneakerless foot out from behind your leg. Let your audience notice it by themselves. What a silly trick! Wouldn't it be great for a clown magician to do?

AND NOW FOR A MIRACLE.

(IT WILL BE A MIRACLE IF THIS TRICK WORKS!)

The Trick

You point to a button on your shirt. "Would you like to see how a magician sews on a button?" you ask. When someone in the audience answers yes, you pull the button off and show it in your hand. "Now watch," you say as you turn your back to the audience. Ten seconds later you turn around again. The button is sewed back in place. Anyone can tug hard on it. Did you really sew it back in ten seconds?

Here's How

Before your audience arrives, take two buttons that match your shirt buttons. Fasten them together with a loop of thin thread. Unbutton one of your shirt buttons. Push half of the secret double button through the buttonhole. Now it looks as if your shirt is buttoned.

When you perform the trick, pull off half of the double button. The other half will drop down inside your shirt. The real button is fastened onto the shirt and hidden under the buttonhole. All you have to do is button the real button through the buttonhole to make it appear in place. Make sure you do this when your back is to the audience.

SEW ON A BUTTON

Tie two buttons back to back with thread.

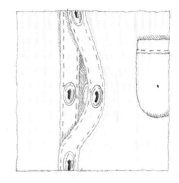

Put one of the double buttons through an unbuttoned buttonhole. Flatten the front of your shirt to make it look as though all your buttons are buttoned.

THE OVER-THE-SINK TRICK

The Trick

Take a plastic glass full of water. Cover it with a handkerchief. Hold the handkerchief in place and tip the glass upside down over a sink. The water runs out. Everyone expects it to.

You repeat the trick. This time you say a magic word: SNARFUGEEZ! Like magic, the water stays inside the glass. It does not run out until you take the handkerchief away.

Here's How

You won't believe this trick until you try it. It works. And it works all by itself, if you do it right.

Fill a plastic glass almost full of water. Cover it with a handkerchief and let the edges fall down around the glass. Put your hand around the glass so the handkerchief is held on like a cover. Turn the glass OVER ALL THE WAY, quickly. The water will not come out if you hold the glass straight up. If you tip the glass, a little water will come out. But it won't come out if you hold the glass straight up. With a little practice you can make the water do anything you want!

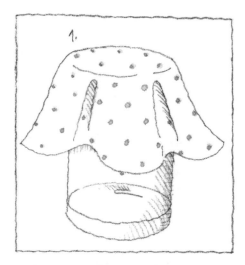

Put a handkerchief over a glass of water.

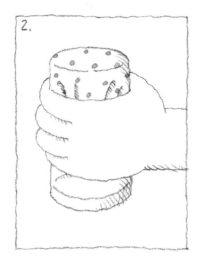

Grip the glass. Your hand should hold the handkerchief on like a cover.

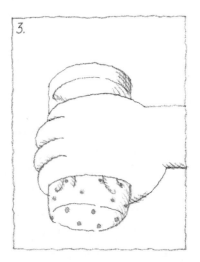

Turn the glass straight upside down, and surprise! No water pours out.

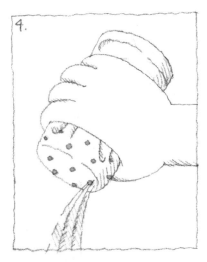

Tip the glass on an angle and water spills out.

MONEY JUST RUNS THROUGH YOUR HAND

The Trick

Hold a penny in your right hand. Show it to your audience. Make a fist with your left hand. Rub your right fist, with the penny in it, against the back of your left fist. Show your audience your right hand again. It is empty! Show them your left hand. The penny is inside! You must have rubbed it through.

Here's How

Follow the above instructions to where you are rubbing the penny against your fist. Now you must do your "trick." Pretend to drop the penny. Let it fall to the floor. Reach down and pick it up with your LEFT hand. Pretend to put it back in your right hand, but really keep it hidden in your left. Practice this part of the trick until you can do it smoothly.

Make your left hand into a fist, with the penny inside. People will think the penny is in your right hand. Rub your right hand against your fist. Rub hard. Pretend you are rubbing the penny through. Slowly open your right hand to show the coin is gone. Slowly open your left fist to show the penny. People will not remember that you dropped the penny earlier.

The Trick

Put a handful of pennies on the table. Have one of your friends select a penny and mark it with a pencil. Drop all the pennies into a paper bag. Ask your friend to shake the bag to mix them up.

Say, "I will reach in and find the marked penny. I'll even tell you how I do this trick. When you made the pencil mark, you put some pencil lead on the penny. That made the penny a bit heavier. All I have to do is find the heaviest penny."

You reach in the bag. You feel around a bit. Then you take out the marked coin!

Here's How

GUM—not weight—is the secret. Before performing the trick, stick a tiny piece of gum on the tip of your thumb. When your friend has finished marking the penny, pick it up between your finger and thumb. Give it a squeeze to make the gum stick to it. Then drop it into the bag. The penny will be easy to find, no matter how mixed up it is with the other pennies.

Rub off the gum before you take the penny out of the bag. And, one last tip: don't use too many pennies, or you'll have a hard time finding the gummed one.

HEAVY PENNY

YOU THINK YOU KNOW THE SECRET BEHIND THIS TRICK? —YOU'RE RIGHT—BUT DON'T TELL ANYONE!

THIS MAGAZINE OFFERS FREE SAMPLES

WATCH MY HANDS CAREFULLY—
YOU'LL NOTICE THAT THEY
NEVER LEAVE MY ARMS.

The Trick

Show your audience a magazine. Flip through it so that people can see the different pages. Shake it to prove there's nothing inside. Roll the magazine into a tube. Reach into the tube. PRESTO! You pull out a handkerchief. "Where did this come from?" you ask.

Here's How

You need an old magazine and some paste or glue. Before your audience arrives, put some glue around the bottom and side edges of the first page. Do not put glue around the top edge. Stick the first page, by the edges, to the cover of the magazine. Be sure to do this smoothly and neatly or you will give yourself away. Let the glue dry. You have just made a secret pocket behind the cover.

Put a handkerchief inside the pocket and flatten it. Now you can show the magazine to your audience. Flip through the pages. Roll the magazine into a tube, with the cover inside. Reach in the top of the tube and grasp the hidden handkerchief. Pull it out and wave it in front of your audience.

1.

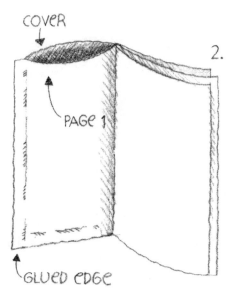

Put glue on the bottom and side edges of page 1.

2.

COVER

PAGE 1

GLUED EDGE

Stick page 1 to the cover to form a pocket. Let the glue dry.

3.

POCKET

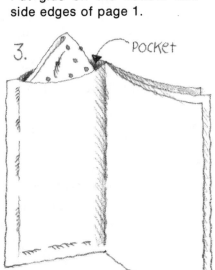

Put a handkerchief inside the pocket and flatten it. Don't let the handkerchief show.

4.

PULL OUT

Roll the magazine into a tube, with the cover on the inside. Reach in and pull out the handkerchief.

THE WATER WIZARD

The Trick

Show both sides of a piece of aluminum foil to your audience. Say, "I am a water wizard. I can get water from anything." Roll the piece into a ball. Squeeze it. Water dribbles out!

Here's How

Take a piece of aluminum foil that's about three inches wide and six inches long. It should be free of holes. Fold it in half. Then fold over the edges twice, leaving one edge open so that you have a pouch. Squeeze along all edges to be sure they are sealed tightly.

Put a big spoonful of water inside the pocket. Fold the open edge over twice, too. You now have a flat bag with a little water inside. Because the foil is stiff, it will appear to be flat. You can show both sides of the foil pouch if you show them quickly. Just be sure your friends don't get too close. From a little ways back they won't be able to see the folded edges.

To do the trick, roll the foil into a ball. Then squeeze. Water surprise from a water wizard!

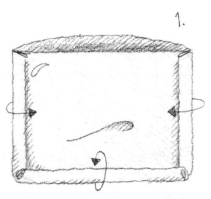

1.

Fold a piece of aluminum foil in half. Fold over the bottom and side edges twice to form a pouch.

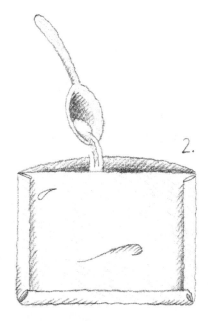

2.

Put a spoonful of water into the pouch.

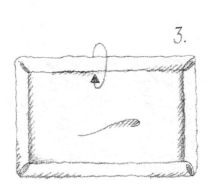

3.

Fold the top edge over twice.

4.

Roll the foil up into a ball and squeeze.

I WILL HYPNOTIZE YOU

The Trick

Show an empty shoebox and ten small cards to a friend. Each card has a different person's name written on it. Read each card out loud and then drop it into the box. Put the cover on the box and shake it to mix the cards. Then say, "My favorite name is MARY MOTHERHEN. It is written on one of the cards in the box. I will hypnotize you and make you find it." You wave your hands mysteriously at your friend and then open the box. Your friend reaches in and, without looking, takes out a card. It says MARY MOTHERHEN.

Here's How

Before your audience arrives, cut a piece of cardboard to fit inside the cover of the box. The cardboard should fit loosely inside the lid. Print MARY MOTHERHEN on ten cards. Place these ten cards inside the cover of the box and put the piece of cardboard over them. Set the lid topside down on a table.

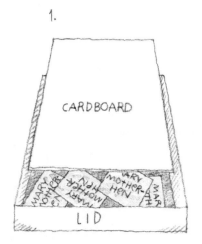

Write MARY MOTHERHEN on ten cards. Put them in the lid of the box. Put a piece of cardboard over them.

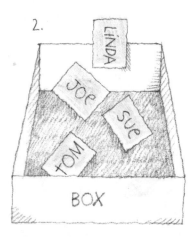

Put ten cards with different names into the box.

30

Make up ten more cards, with MARY MOTHERHEN on one and different names on the other nine. These are the ten names you will read and drop into the box. When you've finished reading the names, put the cover on the box and shake it.

The cardboard piece holding the ten MARY MOTHERHEN cards will fall. Take off the lid and hold the box over your friend's head so that he can't see in. When your friend reaches inside, he will get a MARY MOTHERHEN card, no matter which card is chosen!

This trick takes some practice to do smoothly. When you pick up the cover of the box, be sure to put your thumbs against the outside of the lid and your fingers against the cardboard piece inside. Your fingers will hold the cardboard and keep it from falling before you set the lid on top of the box. Try the trick a few times and you'll find the easiest way to do it.

4.

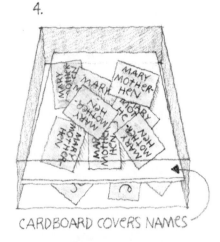

CARDBOARD COVERS NAMES

Pick up the lid to the box. Keep your thumbs on the outside. Your fingers should hold the cardboard piece and keep it from falling too soon. Put the lid on the box.

3.

The piece of cardboard will fall. All the cards on top of the cardboard say MARY MOTHERHEN.

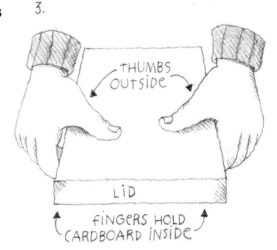

THUMBS OUTSIDE

LID

FINGERS HOLD CARDBOARD INSIDE

GOOD ENOUGH TO DRINK

The Trick

"I'm thirsty," you tell your audience. You flip through a magazine. "Here's a picture of some soda pop," you say. "It's only a picture, but it sure looks good enough to drink." You pick up a drinking glass and tip the top of the magazine over it . . . SWOOSH. You pour real soda out of the magazine.

Here's How

You'll need a plastic sandwich bag, some sticky tape, and an old magazine (it may get wet). A large magazine made of stiff paper will work better than a small, flimsy one.

Before your audience arrives, tape the bag to the middle of the magazine. The opening of the bag should be at the top of the magazine. Use lots of tape. Holding the magazine upright, pour a little soda into the bag. Shut the magazine, but keep it standing up. Prop it up, if necessary, until you're ready to perform the trick.

When your audience arrives, quickly flip through the magazine. Hold it upright and don't let people see the pages. Close the magazine and hold it by the open side. Tip the top over the glass. The soda will pour out. Wet soda coming from a dry magazine is a BIG surprise!

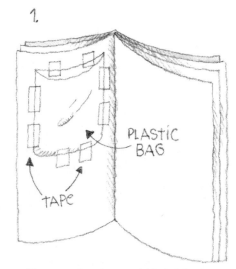

1.

PLASTIC BAG

TAPE

Tape a plastic sandwich bag to the middle of a magazine. The opening of the bag should be at the top of a page.

2.

Hold the magazine upright. Pour some soda into the bag.

3.

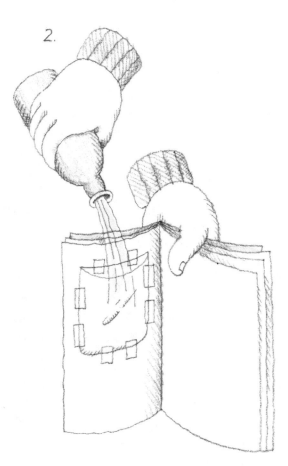

Hold the magazine by the open, or loose, side and pour soda into a glass.

I'LL HUFF AND PUFF

The Trick

You say to your audience, "When I want a certain card, I just blow it out of the deck." Show them a deck of cards. You continue, "For example, if I want the Seven of Spades, I just blow on the bottom of the deck." Hold the deck just above your mouth and blow. The Seven of Spades rises out of the deck!

Here's How

Put the card you want to rise on top of the deck, face down. Now hold the deck up to your face. The top of the deck should touch your forehead. The bottom should stick out just below your nose. The card numbers and suits should face your audience.

Hold a deck of cards up to your face.

Your nose is the secret. Press it against the back of the deck. (It will be against the back of the card you want to rise.) Then begin blowing. Tip your head up and back as you blow. Your nose, not your breath, will push the top card up. The blowing is just to fool your audience.

This trick takes some practice to do well. Practice it in front of a mirror. When you do the trick right, you will probably smile at yourself because you'll look so funny. Then you'll know you've practiced enough to show it to your friends.

Press your nose against the deck and begin blowing.

Tip your head back as you blow. Your nose will push the top card up, but it will look like you are blowing it up.

RED INTO BLUE

The Trick

A small red ball made of crumpled paper and two paper cups are on your table. You drop the ball into one cup. Then you drop that cup into the other cup.

"Hold out your hand," you say to a friend. "I'll bet you can't catch the red ball." You turn the cups upside down over his hand. The ball spills out and he catches it. The ball has turned blue! You say, "I told you that you couldn't catch the red ball!"

Here's How

Before your audience arrives, put a small ball made from crumpled blue paper in one cup. Cut the bottom out of the other cup. Make a crumpled red ball to match the blue one.

When you are ready to perform the trick, show your audience the red ball. Make sure people know it's red by saying so. Pick up the cup with no bottom and set it on your hand. Be careful not to let your audience see there's no bottom in the cup.

He needs to practice!

36

Drop in the red ball as you say, "I will put the red ball in this cup." Lift the cup off your hand. The ball will come out the bottom and stay in your palm. Close your fist around it and drop your arm to your side. Keep looking at the cup as you say, "And I will put the cup into this other cup."

Tell people you have some magic dust in your pocket. You use the hand holding the red ball to reach in your pocket. Leave the ball in your pocket and pretend to get some magic dust. Sprinkle the imaginary dust over the cups. You can now pour out a blue ball from the cups.

One important part of this trick is misdirecting your audience. When the ball is in your hand, be sure to keep your eyes on the cup—not your hand. You might peek in and ask, "What color is the ball?" Your audience will answer, "Red." Nod and say, "You are absolutely right!" By focusing attention on the cup and the color of the ball, you can keep most people from looking at your hand.

AND THE RED BALL HAS TURNED INTO A BLUE BALL... OOPS! STILL RED... WELL, WHAT DO YOU THINK I AM — A MAGICIAN?

SHALL WE TRY ANOTHER TRICK? AS ONE MAGICIAN'S RABBIT SAID TO ANOTHER — LET US.

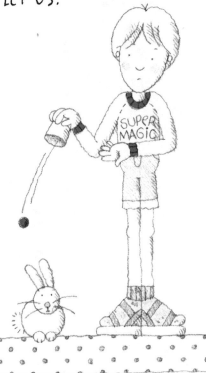

THE ONE-HANDED KNOT

i suppose you think i'm going to take my dog for a walk! actually, i'm going to do a trick with this rope — i call it fatso... but it's been on a diet.

The Trick

You show your audience a piece of rope and say, "Most people need two hands to tie a knot, but I can do it with only one, like this." Drape the rope over your right arm. Hold one end of it with your right hand. Flip the rope off your arm. There is a knot in the middle!

Here's How

Find a piece of rope about as long as you are tall. (You can use a string, but the knot you make will be smaller.) Follow the illustrations to learn exactly how to do the trick.

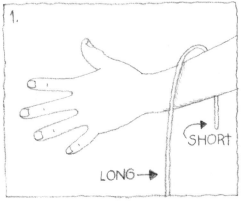

Drape the rope over your right arm. Let the long end of the rope extend down over the left side of your arm.

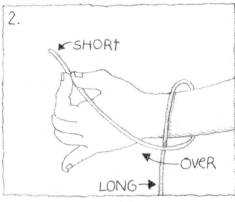

With your left hand, loop the short part around your arm to form a circle. Put the short end in your right hand. Make sure that the short end of the rope crosses over the long end.

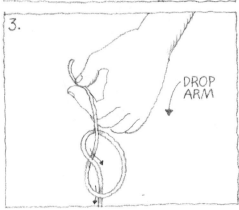

Hold the short end of the rope tight in your hand. Flip the loop off your arm by moving your arm down toward the floor and pulling your hand through the loop. You are still holding the short end of the rope. If you have followed the illustrations carefully, there will be a knot in the middle of the rope. If there is no knot, try again. The trick will seem easy once you can do it right.

THE GREAT PENCIL STICK-CUP

The Trick

Hold a pencil by the eraser so that it is parallel to the floor. Set the mouth of a paper cup on top of the pencil. Take your hand off the cup and balance it on top of the pencil. Slowly turn the pencil over. The cup will stick to the bottom of the pencil!

Separate the cup and pencil and hand them to your audience. People can try the trick. But, of course, it won't work and they won't find out your secret!

Here's How

A loop of thin white thread is needed. Before your audience arrives, tie the thread around the cup, as shown in the illustration. The thread should fit tightly enough so that it won't fall off, but loosely enough so that a pencil can be placed between it and the cup. The cup and the pencil used should also be white, to make the thread invisible from a little ways off.

Put a piece of thread around a cup.

Turn the cup upside down and tilt it toward you so you can see the thread underneath.

40

Make sure that you don't stand too close to the audience. Begin performing the trick by holding the cup upside down. Be careful not to show the mouth of the cup, or the thread might be spotted.

Tilt the cup slightly toward you so that you can see the thread going across the opening. Slip the pencil in under the thread. Hold the cup on top of the pencil with your hand. Then take your hand away from the cup and balance it on top of the pencil. Turn the pencil to flip the cup over. The cup will appear to cling to the bottom of the pencil.

When you separate the cup and the pencil, slide the thread off the cup and let it fall to the floor. Now nobody (not even you) can do the trick.

Flip the cup over. It will cling to the pencil.

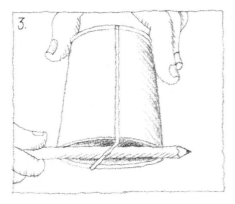

Slip a pencil under the thread.

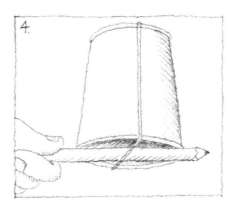

Show the cup balanced on the pencil.

THE WIZARD'S RING

The Trick

Hold up a finger ring and say to your audience, "This is a wizard's ring. I'll show you why. Do you see it?" Yes, your audience will answer. "No, you don't!" you say. You show them both of your hands. The wizard's ring has vanished!

Here's How

You will need a plastic finger ring and three rubber bands. And you must wear a long-sleeved shirt with open cuffs. Loop the bands and the ring together. To do this, follow the directions given in the top illustration on the next page.

Slip band C around your wrist and under your shirt. Slip it far back, over your elbow. Stretch out the other two bands and hold the ring in your hand. Keep your palm and the rubber bands hidden from view.

After showing the ring, pretend to toss it into the air. When you move your hand, let the ring go. The rubber band will pull it up your sleeve, and your hand will be left empty.

Practice this trick while looking in a mirror. When you do it right, the ring will disappear so fast you will even fool yourself!

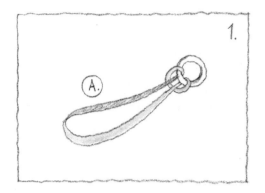

1.

To loop together band *A* and the ring, overlap the ring with the end of *A*. Push the end of *A* through the ring and around through *A*. Pull on the end of *A*.

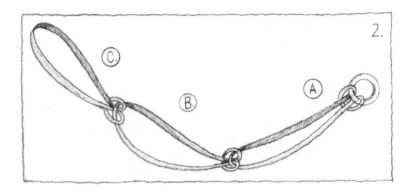

2.

In the same way, loop band *A* around band *B*. Then loop together bands *B* and *C*.

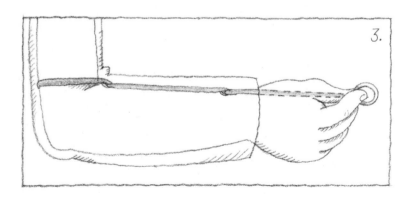

3.

Slip band *C* around your wrist and up over your elbow. Stretch out the other two bands and hold the ring in your hand. Toss the ring up. The bands pull it up your shirt sleeve. Hint: Only show the back of your hand and arm to your audience. Keep the bands hidden in your palm.

THE MAGIC LINKING CLIPS

The Trick

Fold a long strip of paper in half. Loop a rubber band over the strip near the crease. Put a paper clip over the middle of the folded strip. Fold the front half of the strip over again. Place another clip over the paper near the first fold. Pull hard on the two ends of the paper. ZWIP! The two paper clips and the rubber band are linked together!

Here's How

Follow the illustrations carefully. If the trick doesn't work for you, you may not be clipping the clips properly. Remember that each one should hold two layers of paper, not just one or all three. If your paper keeps tearing, try again using a strip of thicker paper.

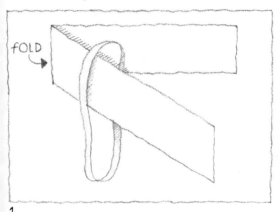

1. Fold a long strip of thick paper in half. Loop a rubber band over the middle near the crease.

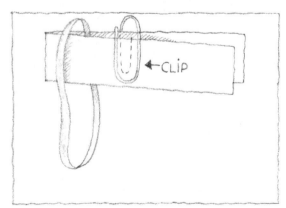

2. Clip the middle of the folded strip. Make sure that the clip goes over both layers of paper.

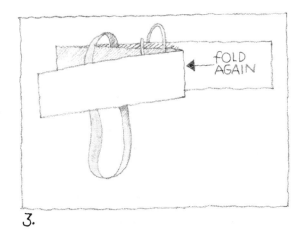

Fold the front half of the paper over again, toward you.

3.

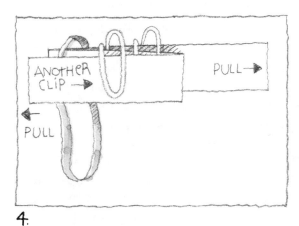

Clip the second clip over the top two layers of paper. The band should be to the left of the second clip. Pull hard on the ends of the strip.

4.

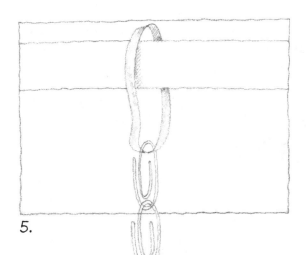

The paper clips and the rubber band should be linked together over the paper.

5.

THE FANTASTIC FLYING FOULARD

The Trick

You remove the handerchief from your pocket. You toss it down on the floor and shout, "Fly!" You wave your arms. Amazing—the handkerchief flies off the floor and into your hand!

Here's How

Before you perform this trick, get some thread that matches the color of your pants or dress. Cut off a piece that's just a little longer than the distance from the floor to your waist. Tie one end of the thread to your belt. Tie the other end to a corner of the handkerchief. Put the handkerchief in your pocket.

To perform the trick, remove the handkerchief and toss it on the floor. Loop your thumb under the top of the thread by your belt. Order your handkerchief to fly. Quickly lift both of your arms. Make sure that you lift the hand with the thread straight up. The handkerchief will be lifted right up to your hand!

Do the trick quickly. You will surprise everybody. People will see the handkerchief flying before they have time to look for the thread.

This makes a great trick to end your magic show. After the handkerchief is in your hand, wave it up and down. Say, "Goodbye and thank you for watching my tricks."

Oh, and by the way, a "foulard" is a fancy handkerchief.

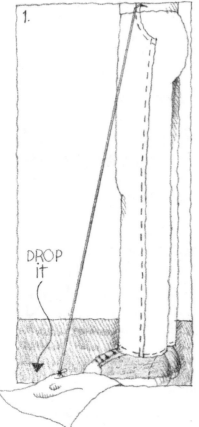

Take a handkerchief out of your pocket and toss it on the floor. The handkerchief should be attached to your belt by a string.

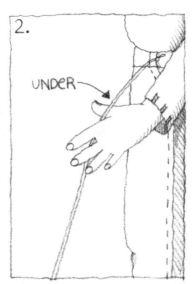

Put your thumb under the thread near your belt.

Lift both of your arms straight up. The handkerchief will appear to fly to your hands.

GOODBYE—
AND REMEMBER,
MAGIC IS
CIGAM
SPELLED
BACKWARDS!

RAY BROEKEL has written and edited over a hundred books for children. He has been interested in performing magic for about twenty-five years, ever since he and Laurence White first met. His favorite trick involves using a piece of magic chalk that can write any color.

Ray Broekel lives with his wife in Ipswich, Massachusetts. They have two grown children.

LAURENCE WHITE, JR., started doing magic tricks when he was in first grade. He was soon earning his spending money by putting on magic shows. Today he says that he wishes he still had all the money he earned from his childhood performances.

Author of many science and magic books for children, Laurence White serves as the Director of the Science Center for the Needham, Massachusetts, schools. He and his wife, Doris, and their two sons, Bill and Dave, live in Stoughton, Massachusetts.

MARY THELEN has wide experience in art and design. She has been an art director for a small midwestern press, an assistant art director for a greeting cards company, and an illustrator for an advertising firm. She has written and designed two books of her own.

2

9/99